MW00619169

Find Out what is your Day Master with your phone/browser

1. Go to **www.joeyyap.com/DM**

2. Key in your Date of Birth

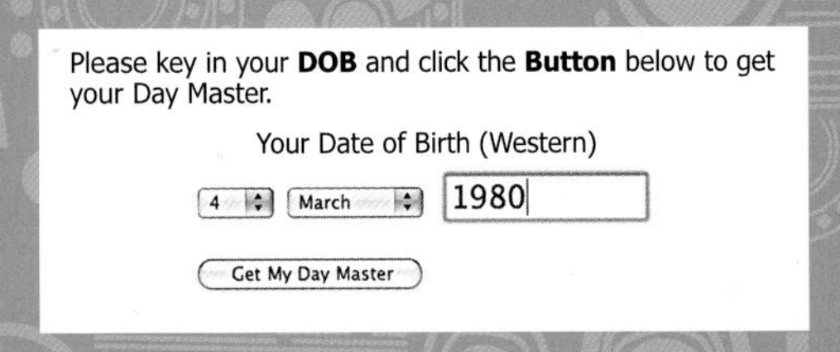

3. Your Day Master is instantly revealed

Your Day Master is:

DING

YIN FIRE

* The calculator will automatically convert your Western date of birth to Chinese in deriving your Day Master

DING
YIN FIRE

BaZi Essentials: The Ten Day Masters - Ding Fire

First Edition July 2009

The author can be reached at:

Mastery Academy of Chinese Metaphysics Sdn. Bhd. (611143-A)
19-3, The Boulevard, Mid Valley City,
59200 Kuala Lumpur, Malaysia.
Tel : +603-2284 8080
Fax : +603-2284 1218
Website : www.masteryacademy.com

Published by JY Books Sdn. Bhd. (659134-T)

INDEX

MASTERY ACADEMY
OF CHINESE METAPHYSICS™

At **www.masteryacademy.com**, you will find some useful tools to ascertain key information about the Feng Shui of a property or for the study of Astrology.

The Joey Yap Flying Stars Calculator can be utilised to plot your home or office Flying Stars chart. To find out your personal best directions, use the 8 Mansions Calculator. To learn more about your personal Destiny, you can use the Joey Yap BaZi Ming Pan Calculator to plot your Four Pillars of Destiny – you just need to have your date of birth (day, month, year) and time of birth.

For more information about BaZi, Xuan Kong or Flying Star Feng Shui, or if you wish to learn more about these subjects with Joey Yap, logon to the Mastery Academy of Chinese Metaphysics website at **www.masteryacademy.com.**

MASTERY ACADEMY
E-LEARNING CENTER

www.maelearning.com

Bookmark this address on your computer, and visit this newly-launched website today. With the E-Learning Center, knowledge of Chinese Metaphysics is a mere 'click' away!

Our E-Learning Center consists of 3 distinct components.

1. Online Courses
These shall comprise of 3 Programs: our Online Feng Shui Program, Online BaZi Program, and Online Mian Xiang Program. Each lesson contains a video lecture, slide presentation and downloadable course notes.

2. MA Live!
With MA Live!, Joey Yap's workshops, tutorials, courses and seminars on various Chinese Metaphysics subjects broadcasted right to your computer screen. Better still, participants will not only get to see and hear Joey talk 'live', but also get to engage themselves directly in the event and more importantly, TALK to Joey via the MA Live! interface. All the benefits of a live class, minus the hassle of actually having to attend one!

3. Video-On-Demand (VOD)
Get immediate streaming-downloads of the Mastery Academy's wide range of educational DVDs, right on your computer screen. No more shipping costs and waiting time to be incurred!

Study at your own pace, and interact with your Instructor and fellow students worldwide...at your own convenience and privacy. With our E-Learning Center, knowledge of Chinese Metaphysics is brought DIRECTLY to you in all its clarity, with illustrated presentations and comprehensive notes expediting your learning curve!

Welcome to the Mastery Academy's E-LEARNING CENTER...
YOUR virtual gateway to Chinese Metaphysics mastery!

DING
YIN FIRE

Akin to the fire of a gently flickering candle, lamp, or torch.

INTRODUCTION :
THE BASICS OF BAZI - THE TEN DAY MASTERS

Why BaZi Essentials?

BaZi (八字) is system of Chinese Astrology known as the Four Pillars of Destiny. BaZi literally translates to mean 'Eight Characters,' because the eight characters are derived from four pairs of characters – hence, the four pillars. BaZi translates our birth information – specifically the year, month, day, and hour of birth into four pillars known as Jia Zi. And what are these Eight Characters? They are made up of the Yin and Yang variations of the Five Elements (Wood, Water, Metal, Fire and Earth).

The idea for the **BaZi Essentials** series of books began out of my wish to simplify what is a sophisticated, multifaceted study of authentic Chinese Astrology into something a little easier to digest. Too many people are only familiar with the "12 Animal Year Signs" type of Chinese Astrology. But the true form of character traits in Chinese Astrology stems from the Day of Birth, not the animal sign of the Year of Birth.

If you've read my previous books on BaZi, ***BaZi – The Destiny Code*** and ***BaZi – The Destiny Code Revealed***, or even taken any classes on the subject, you probably know that there is really NO end to BaZi studies. There may be a finite amount of theory or principles to learn, but the methods of application and interpretation are endless. And that's precisely why BaZi is a consistently intriguing and exciting field of Destiny study!

But every form of knowledge has to start somewhere. And BaZi essentially begins with the Day Master, or the Day Stem. This is basically – **YOUR DAY OF BIRTH**. On your BaZi chart, as shown in the image below, the Day Master refers to the 'Heavenly Stem' section of your Day Pillar.

時 Hour	日 Day	月 Month	年 Year	
	丁 Ding **Yin Fire**			天干
				地支 Earthly

If you don't know what's your chart or your Day Master, no problem – you can log on to my website at http://www.joeyyap.com/bazi to plot your BaZi chart.

The Heavenly Stems on the BaZi chart are denoted by the upper halves of each of the four pillars, while the bottom halves are known as the Earthly Branches. Heavenly Stems represent what is known as surface Qi. In essence, the Heavenly Stems reveal what you are on the exterior or the 'outside' – your personality or character traits that are visible to everyone who knows you. When people say, "He's stubborn" or "She's extremely friendly," these are the characteristics that are visible to others, and it is seen on the Heavenly Stems.

The Earthly Branches (meaning, the animal signs in the Year, Month, Day and Hour pillars), in contrast, indicate what is *inside* a person. These are hidden, sometimes buried, personality traits and characteristics – and are only known to others once you truly get to know a person. Sometimes, it may even take up to years before some of these traits are discovered by others!

There are 10 Heavenly Stems, or Day Masters, in BaZi study. These 10 Stems comprise the Yin and Yang aspects of the Five Elements of Chinese Metaphysics: Wood, Fire, Earth, Metal, and Water. For every element, there is a Yin and Yang polarity, giving us ten Stems in total.

The Day Master is the most important reference point for BaZi analysis. Before you can go anywhere with using BaZi to analyse your life, you begin with the Day Master – which denotes your basic nature and character. It denotes WHO YOU ARE at the most fundamental level. Therefore, it follows that people who are of the same Day Master share similar traits.

The BaZi Essentials Series has ten books, with each one focusing on one individual Day Master. This book that you have in your hands is on the Yin Fire, or Ding Fire, Day Master. (To better immerse yourself in BaZi, use the proper terminology. So, if you're a Ding Fire Day Master, refer to yourself as a "Ding Fire person" instead of "Yin Fire person.")

Shining a candle on Ding Fire

Clearly, if you're a Ding Fire Day Master, you are more than just a human representation of a strongly burning sun! While you will exhibit the most obvious and general qualities of the Ding Fire Day Master to a greater or lesser degree, you may also demonstrate different attributes in different situations.

What are your most basic personality traits? What are you like in your career, in your relationships, and how do you deal with money? What type of entrepreneur or businessperson are you likely to be? What type of person are you in the workplace, and how do you operate as a leader or manager? What kind of friend or colleague are you?

All these questions and more are addressed in this book, so that you're able to see exactly how the Ding Fire person operates in various aspects of his or her life. While there are other factors to consider when analysing a person's fundamental character, motivations in life, and outlook and destiny, a Ding Fire person's modus operandi, so to speak, is significantly different from the other Day Masters.

How Ding (丁) are you?

If you're a Ding Fire Day Master, you are likely to exhibit the majority of the traits that is highlighted in the book. If you're not a Ding Fire Day Master but you have the Ding Fire as one (or more) of the Heavenly Stems in your BaZi chart, then you're likely to exhibit these tendencies in lesser degrees. Alternatively, it suggests that you have the potential or inclination to exhibit these tendencies in *specific* situations and contexts only.

In BaZi, the concept of STRONG or WEAK elements plays a big role in determining how 'Ding' you are.

So bear in mind that even if you are a Ding Fire Day Master, whether or not you display the traits covered here to a greater or lesser degree depends very much on the strength and quality of your Day Master. The Day Stem is but one part of the chart, and there are 3 other Stems and 4 Earthly Branches to consider in your complete chart. These other parts of the chart will influence the strength and quality of your Day Master.

These factors are too varied and complex to be discussed here in a simple book (it is, however, a fundamental section of my professional BaZi courses and Destiny Code series of books). Suffice to say that to read and understand this particular book, you merely need to be aware of this concept. If your Day Master is strong, you'll exhibit MORE of these tendencies or traits outlined in the book. If your Day Master is weak, you'll exhibit less of these traits.

Do keep in mind that this book shows you the traits of the Ding Fire Day Master *in general*, and doesn't take into account the particularities of your entire BaZi chart! Having said that, nothing beats getting a complete BaZi consultation from a professional, or taking a full BaZi course and learning the interpretation skills completely for yourself.

BaZi Astrology is a study that helps us understand ourselves, make better decisions, and ultimately, enables us to shape our life for the better. With these pocket-sized books, I hope to make BaZi a relevant a part of your life – and may the knowledge that you gain serve you in all of life's endeavours.

All the best in your BaZi studies... and here's to discovering what the Ding Fire person is all about!

Joey Yap
July 2009

Author's personal websites :
www.joeyyap.com I www.fengshuilogy.com (Personal blog)

Academy websites :
www.masteryacademy.com I www.masteryjournal.com I www.maelearning.com

Follow Joey's current updates on Twitter :
www.twitter.com/joeyyap

CHARACTER

人格
personality

PERSONALITY

GENTLE AND REFINED

A candle in the wind

Ding Fire is Yin Fire. If you want to envision what Ding Fire looks like, think of the subtle, quiet fire from a gently flickering candle, torch, or lamp. Ding Fire is restrained fire, as opposed to the blazing brightness of the sun. Ding Fire people, likewise, are often discreet, elegant souls.

Their characters are not usually loud, and their personalities are not usually rough. In most cases, Ding Fire people are refined, attractive, polite, courteous, and gracious, and possess a slight conservative air about them. They may look quiet and calm on first impressions.

That's how a candle looks. But once you get to know them, they are usually the types to be laughing heartily and making jokes, and may become the life of the party.

Ding Fire people are also very refined and sophisticated, and will pay careful attention to all that they say and do. They are often considerate of others and will place significant emphasis on being caring and understanding of others' needs and desires.

KEY FACTS

- **Possess courteous manners**
- **Mild, polished, and cultured**
- **Considerate and kind**
- **Meticulous**
- **Subtle and understated**

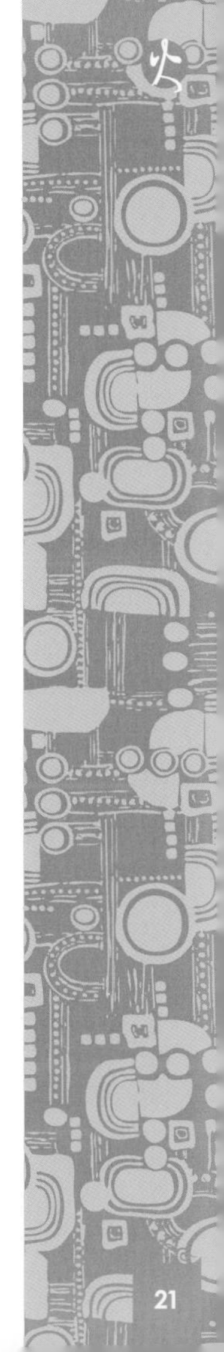

PHILOSOPHICAL

Thinkers who are keen to learn

Ding Fire people are, by nature, sensitive thinkers who love to ponder over a juicy intellectual problem. They can, however, be a bit too sensitive at times and be prone to worrying and fretting. In some cases, they are given to over-analysing a situation or problem.

They are always open to learning new things, be it the traditional way of hitting the books, or through exposure to new and varied life experiences. They are attracted to knowledge. They are open to fresh ideas, perceptions, and observations, and will enjoy giving their mind a good workout.

Ding Fire minds are naturally given to being detail-oriented and precise, and they also enjoy leading the way and showing others the path forward. Their knowledge-seeking ways are closely tied to their interest in inspiring and illuminating other people, just like the single fiery spark that sets the tinder alight.

KEY FACTS

- Thoughtful
- Intelligent
- Keen on inspiring others
- Enjoy absorbing new knowledge
- Sensitive and receptive

TEMPERAMENTAL

Can leave destruction in their wake

Just like the fire from a candle flickers according to the strength and direction of the wind, Ding Fire people have the potential to be very volatile and easily upset where their emotions are concerned. One minute they can be calm and pleasant, and the very next they could be raging mad!

In that same vein, they can go from being very patient and organised to being very rash and impulsive within a short frame of time. While they're careful, they're not apt to being consistent. At times, their sensitivity renders them prickly and excessively touchy.

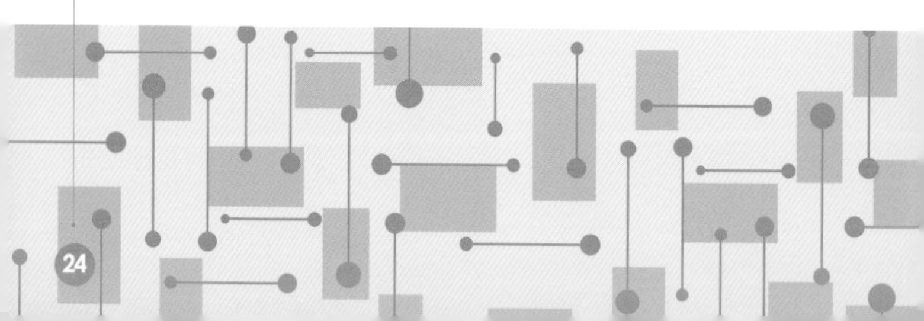

Because their emotions can be unstable for the most part, they may be prone to being easily suspicious of others, and as a result, may be hyper-vigilant. This lends their interpersonal connections a sense of imbalance or uncertainty. You can never be entirely sure-footed around a Ding Fire person.

KEY FACTS

- Volatile
- Fickle-minded
- Impulsive at times
- Unstable
- Touchy

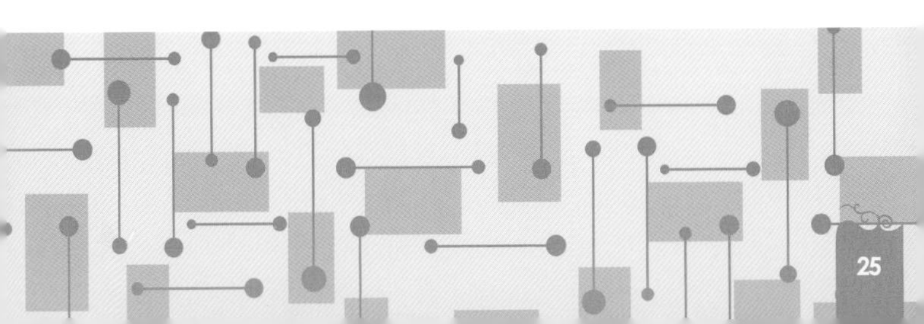

DEVOTED AND AFFECTIONATE

Putting others ahead of themselves

Ding Fire may not be able to radiate warmth to the far corners of the world, but when warmth is needed, a candle or torch can provide enough to the people who need it. Likewise, Ding Fire people are extremely loyal, devoted, and loving to the people to whom they're close.

Ding Fire individuals, more than any other Day Master, exhibit qualities of 'filial piety' towards their parents, especially their mother. They are willing to make sacrifices to those nearest and dearest, and will tend to place the needs of others ahead of their own.

As such, at times they need to be reminded that they have their own desires and wishes to consider. They are, however, very good at downplaying themselves when the situation calls for it, while waiting for the right opportunity to shine again when the time is right.

KEY FACTS ■■■

- **Self-sacrificial for loved ones**
- **Giving and caring**
- **Respectful to parents**
- **Filial**
- **Loving**

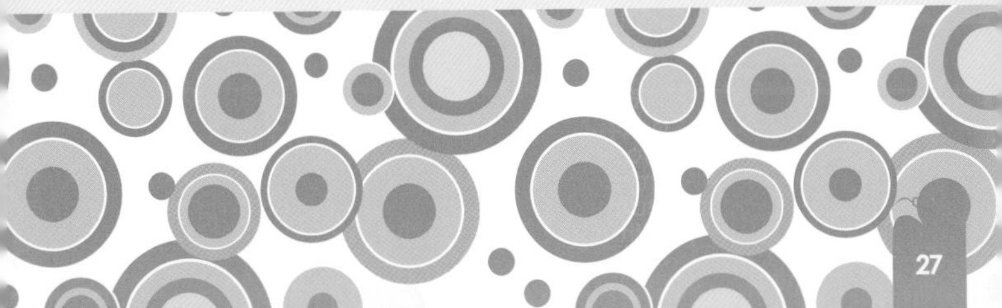

判斷
judgment

THINKING & JUDGMENT

DETAILED AND THOROUGH

Exploring issues from every angle

Ding Fire people are very detailed and thorough in their thinking, regardless of whether the matter is big or small. It doesn't matter if something is important or trivial, Ding Fire people will take care of the issue! The way that fire consumes everything it burns. They are the type of people who will go all out to ensure that every problem is solved in a smooth manner that is agreeable to all.

They have a style that is consistently calm and steady on the outside, but internally they rarely break away from the traditional style of thinking. Ding Fire people prefer to adhere to the

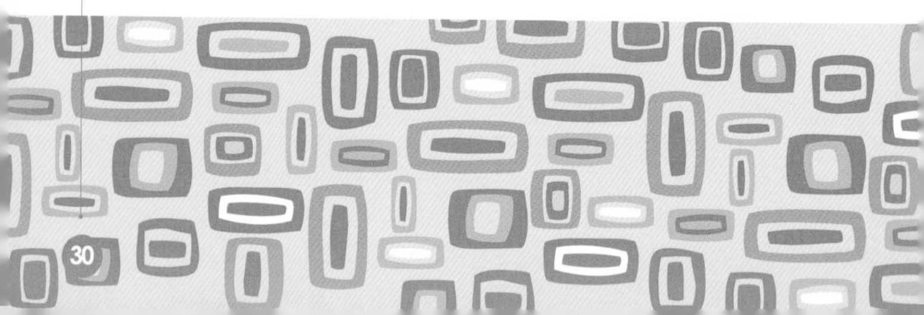

cautious, old-school mode of thinking. However, they are still able to approach each issue from different angles and perspectives. It's just that they don't quite like to shake things up thoroughly from the inside out.

They may take a little more time than usual in getting things done, but one can rest assured that the problem or situation will have been explored from every angle. Ding Fire people are not usually the type to leave a problem hanging or dangling. As such, they often have the ability to penetrate to the source or heart of any issue.

KEY FACTS

- **Exhaustive and precise**
- **Firm and steady when problem-solving**
- **Considers all angles**
- **Has multiple perspectives**

TRUST NO ONE
The constant questioner

Ding Fire people are not wholly accepting of unrefuted traditional viewpoints, and will have a tendency to question the more accepted forms of thought. Opinions and perspectives that are not supported by facts and proofs will be harshly criticised by Ding Fire people. Don't try to fob off any unsubstantiated outrageous claims on them!

They enjoy learning and doing research with people with whom they share the same thoughts and beliefs. They enjoy forming learning groups with people and sharing their respective thoughts and ideas with each other. But the only drawback is that they tend to share with people who are of the same leanings as them.

As such, they tend to learn and absorb new things without really shaking up their perceptions or belief system. They can be a little too moderate and conservative in their thoughts, and will prefer to go around in circles in their comfort zone. Thus, they may never really achieve true impartiality or objectivity because of this tendency.

KEY FACTS

- **Strong critic**
- **Want substantiated proof**
- **Enjoy learning things with others**
- **Results-oriented**

FAST DECISION-MAKERS

No waffling about

Ding Fire people tend to make their judgment calls very quickly, and are not given to endlessly musing over or pondering their decisions. However, their swiftness doesn't necessarily guarantee accuracy or precision, and as such they're still capable of making the wrong choices whenever they are hasty.

On the whole, they have their respective measures or yardsticks for evaluating a possible problem or scenario. They

do not spend too much time hesitating over what is going on, and as a result, they don't really have a tendency to waste their time or their resources.

While they are constant skeptics of traditional forms of thought, they prefer adhering to a standard set of principles or terms when it comes to organising their patterns of thought. Ding Fire types are not the kind of people who will let their thoughts be influenced by radical new perceptions or changes.

KEY FACTS

- **Swift**
- **Not given to dawdling**
- **Principled**
- **Given to inaccuracy**

viewpoints

Quick Tips to Develop Strategic Thinking:

- *Brainstorm with other people*
- *Hit the books. Do a lot more research.*
- *Gain newer, different perspectives when trying to make a specific decision*
- *Must be open to distinctive viewpoints, even if those perspectives clash with theirs*
- *Make an effort to be humble, open-minded, and open to criticism*
- *Be ready to apologise for any mistakes or inaccuracies as a result of their quick decision-making*

Some ideas for how Ding Fire people can improve their thinking processes and cultivate their deepest potential:

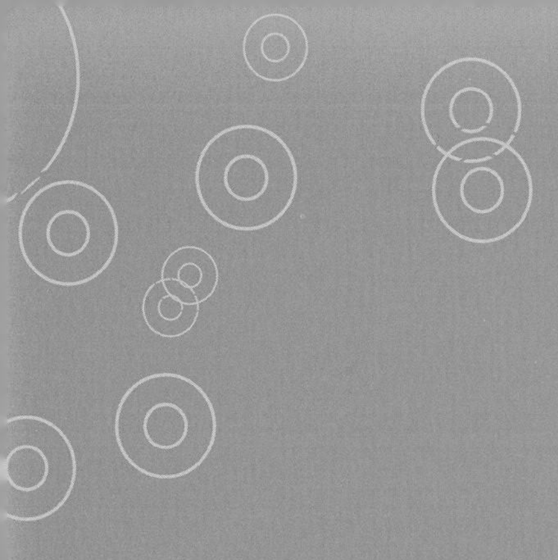

- **Learn all about logic and the philosophy of mind.** It will benefit Ding Fire people to research logic and structural forms of thinking, as learning about these matters can help one think better. It will also allow Ding Fire people to experience new forms of thought processes that will help them formulate their thoughts with more clarity.

- **Learn how to Mind-Map**. An essential brainstorming tool that would prove useful to all Ding Fire people.

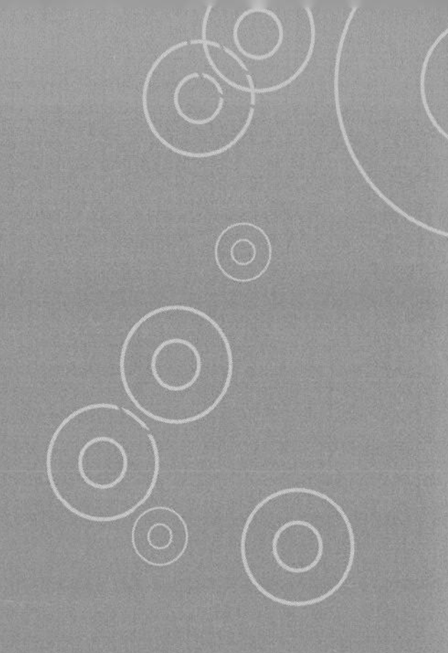

- **Read about different topics.** Ding Fire people should also make an effort to read about topics and subjects that are out of their normal interests. One of the best ways to train oneself to be a thinker is to learn and think about subjects that are not within one's usual realm. By doing this, they can also see the weaknesses in their thoughts and rectify their thinking processes from there.

- **Get the mind jogging.** The right amount of exercise doesn't only benefit the physical body, it also helps to freshen and strengthen the mental faculties. Ding Fire people can try jogging, especially in an area that is peaceful and conducive for letting their mind rest. It doesn't matter if it's fast or slow, but it should be for a long stretch of time and preferably done without any form of pressure or the urge to compete.

- **Affirm their own ability to solve problems.** Every time they're faced with problems, Ding Fire people should look themselves in the mirror and tell themselves that they are able to solve it. This will boost their confidence – and the more confident they are, the better their mental problem-solving skills. Doing this often enough will help to train the Ding Fire mental process.

self-confidence

SELF-CONFIDENCE

GENEROUSLY NURTURING

But excessively self-sacrificial

Ding Fire people are, on the whole, very nurturing and loving, and they want to bring out the best in others. Just remember that the image of Ding Fire is the candle. And candles do burn out to provide light. Where other people are concerned, especially those to whom they're close, Ding Fire types will often put their needs ahead of their own.

This will affect their self-confidence for good or for bad, depending on how other people respond to them. Ding Fire people are by nature nurturers and illuminators who love to guide others and help them out, but just like a candle

that burns out too soon – they must not give away too much of themselves and keep none for their own needs!

Other people who are less principled or simply more manipulative can often take advantage of the Ding Fire's kindness. When they realise this, their self-confidence will take a dip. So Ding Fire people must make an effort to keep their needs and desires on the forefront, as well, and refrain from sacrificing too much for others to their own detriment.

KEY FACTS ■ ■ ■

- **Sacrifice too much to others**
- **May be taken advantage of**
- **Don't express their true needs and wants**
- **Too willing to do things for others**

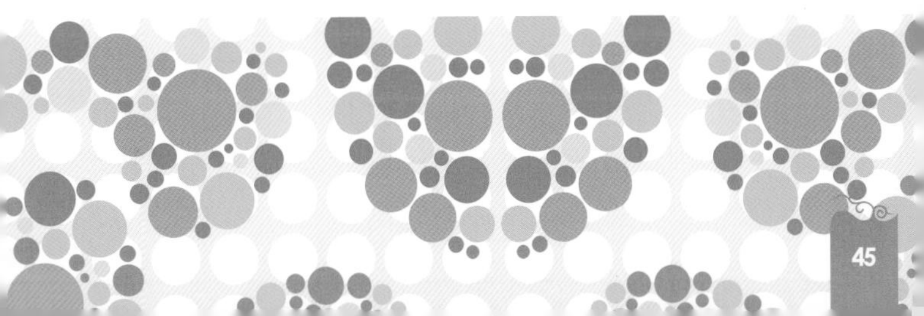

AFRAID OF FAILURE

The only way is success

Ding Fire people are extremely confident in the things they're good at, and will spend a lot of their time on these particular activities. But once they've tried something new and failed it for the first time, they have a tendency to want to avoid doing it again. This is because Ding Fire, the candlelight fire, is fragile in some ways.

Their sense of self is very much tied to being good or successful at something, and failure is not something that the Ding Fire self-confidence can tolerate at all. They do not enjoy learning from

past failures and mistakes. They tend to have high expectations of themselves and often don't realise that failure is an essential step in the path to success.

As a result, and average Ding Fire person tends to risk missing out on some of the richer experiences of life because they are too afraid to fail again. Weaker Ding Fire people tend to think that they will be judged and assessed on their failures, not realising that the value of failure lies in the experience itself, and the lessons they have learned.

KEY FACTS

- **Fear of failing**
- **High premium on succeeding**
- **Will be adversely affected by failure**
- **May miss out on experiences**

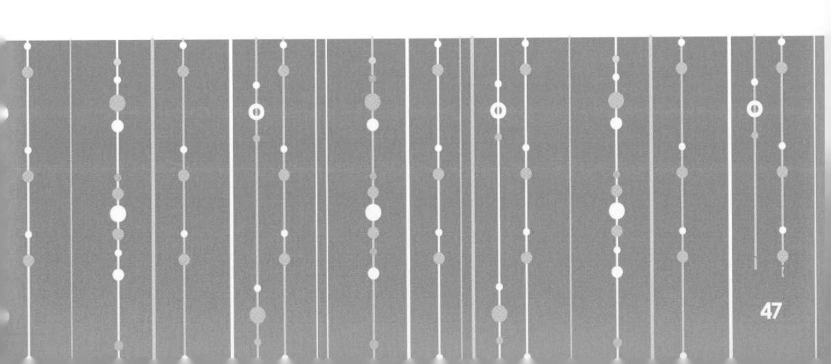

THE PARENT TRAP
Influenced by childhood past

Ding Fire people are one of the few Day Masters keenly affected by their past, and the influences of their childhood. Because they are naturally very filial to their parental figures, they tend to place an immense amount of value on what their parents or family members think of them. This is because as a Yin Fire, it needs to consume 'wood'. Wood is the source of fire. This is akin to a child who needs his/her parents (resource).

As adults, their levels of self-confidence are greatly affected by what has gone in their lives in the past. If they suffered through teasing or trauma in their past, it would have left a big wound in their psyche that will still affect their self-esteem in adulthood.

The more they suffered in terms of teasing or deprecation when they were younger at the hands of their parents or guardians, the more likely they are to be scared and sensitive as adults. Likewise, meaningful experiences during childhood and youth can build a great Ding Fire achiever. Many Ding Fire people often have trouble separating their past experiences from their current ones.

KEY FACTS ■■■

- Influenced by the past
- Keenly affected by childhood experiences
- Parental influence is very strong
- Trauma in the past affects their adult performance

achievements

Quick Tips to Build Self-Confidence:

- *Create achievements in their adult life by focusing on their career and their passions and interests*
- *Find their purpose in life, and do all it takes to achieve that – it will create an unshakeable sense of self*
- *Do the things that give them a sense of fulfillment or contentment from the inside – not in terms of money, material gains, or reputation*
- *Avoid judgmental people*
- *Learn from the past instead of dreading the past*
- *Must realise that the past is a good teacher for a better future*

The Ding Fire Character at a Glance:

- Ding Fire people are generally very refined and elegant, with a subtle presence that doesn't announce itself too loudly. Like a candle, you illuminate your presence in a room.

- You usually possess impeccable manners, and project a very cultured and civilised persona. You're not one to embarrass or shock others with loud, boorish, and coarse behaviour. As such, you will have no problems appealing to the parents of your future spouse when you meet them for the first time!
- Philosophy speaks to your soul, and Plato makes your heart sing! Even if it's not philosophical treatises that interest you, you're very much interested in learning new things. You're always open to gaining new knowledge in any capacity.
- In any problem or situation, you tend to zero in on the finer points and take it from there. You have an eye for precision, and are meticulous in all that you do.

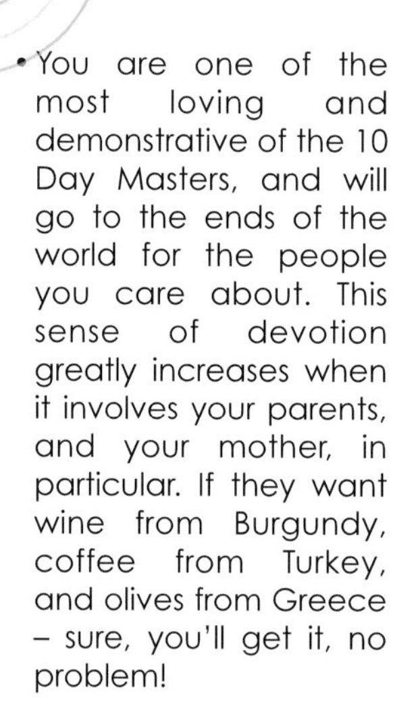

- You are one of the most loving and demonstrative of the 10 Day Masters, and will go to the ends of the world for the people you care about. This sense of devotion greatly increases when it involves your parents, and your mother, in particular. If they want wine from Burgundy, coffee from Turkey, and olives from Greece – sure, you'll get it, no problem!

- When it comes to making decisions, you have a tendency to do it fast. While others are turning over ten different options for places to have dinner, you breeze in with a decision in a matter of seconds.

- But all should beware the wrath of the Ding Fire! Just like an overturned candle can raze a fire through buildings and cause immense destruction, so can you blaze a trail of ruin behind you when your fury has been ignited.

- You can be mercurial and temperamental. If your colleagues see you smiling in the morning when you enter the office, they cannot be certain that you will even pull a muscle in your face when they approach you a few hours later.

- Whether you were the nerd, the athletic one, or the popular one in your childhood, it will greatly influence how you operate as an adult.

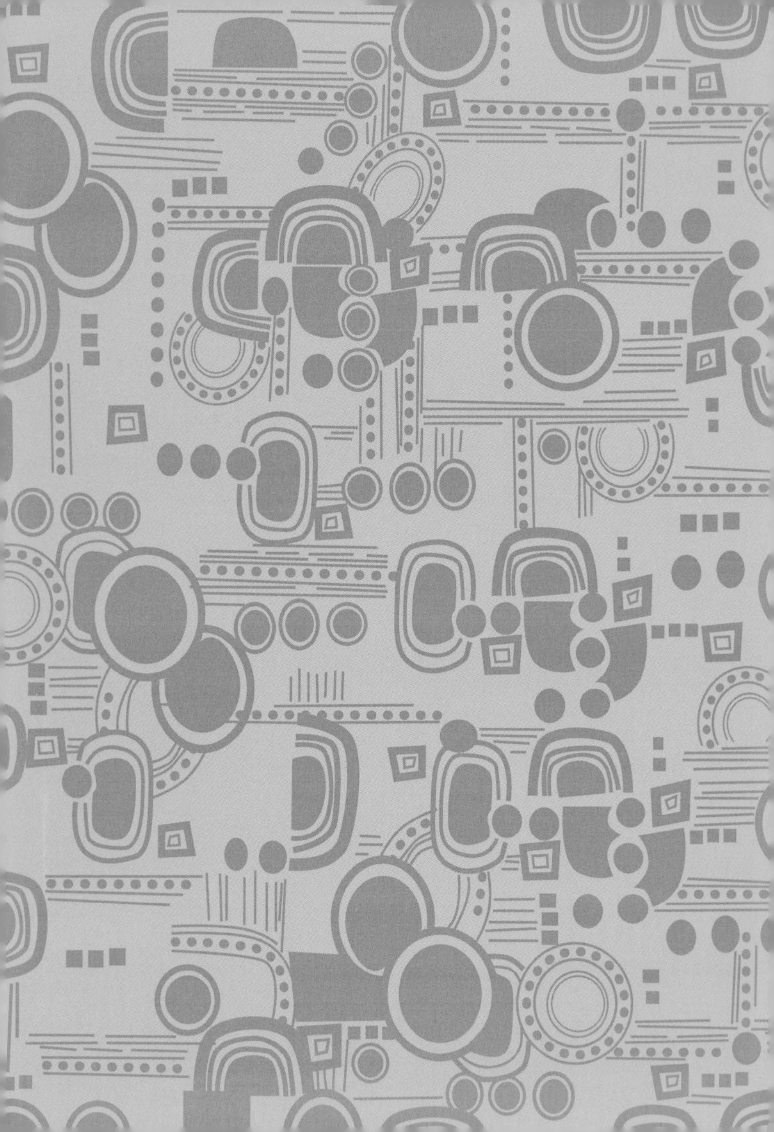

CAREER

領導
lead

WORK PERSONALITY & LEADERSHIP

TOLERANT
Amiable and helpful

At work, Ding Fire people often gain plenty of brownie points for being extremely helpful, affable, and cordial. There is no request or favour that they will not grant. Others will often find it easy to come to the Ding Fire person for help and assistance, as they will be ones in the workplace who will be most willing to give it.

Sometimes, they may even do this at their own expense. They will neglect to fulfill their own desires or needs, and will not be so forthcoming in asking for help. Giving help? No problem at all. Asking for it? That's another issue entirely!

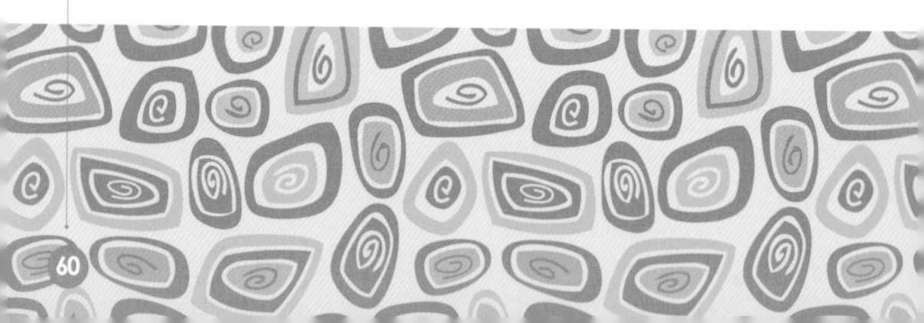

Possessing good manners and courtesy, Ding Fire people are usually very welcome in any work environment. They are pleasant and they keep the peace, and are not the rebellious outlaws who are always causing trouble for other people!

KEY FACTS

- **Ready to lend a helping hand**
- **Appreciated by everyone**
- **Pleasant personality**
- **Courteous and civil**

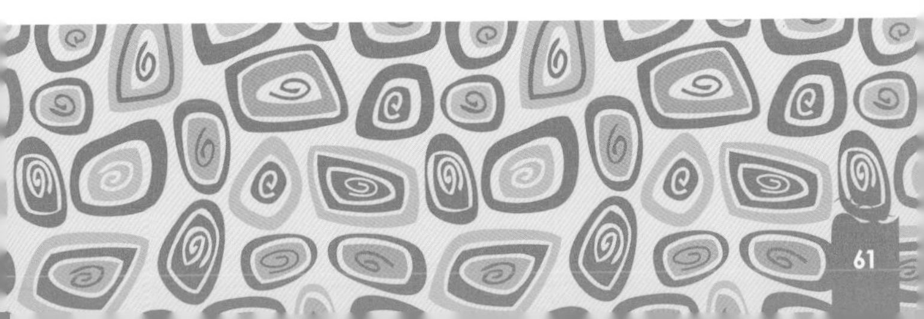

DORMANT TALENT

But a trailblazer once they get going

Consider the candle or a torch – before it is even lit, no one is aware of the amount of light and warm it can bring. This is the image of Ding Fire people – they don't display their talents or capabilities from the start. Instead, they tend to lay dormant for awhile before they catch fire.

In the workplace, Ding Fire people may often seem unassuming or unremarkable at first, but this is no means because they lack talent. Most of the time, they simply lurk in the shadows, biding their time before which they can shine forth with confidence.

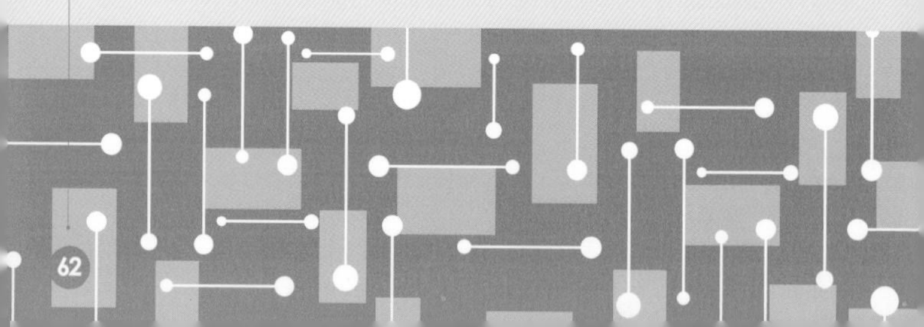

Once they are ready to share their capabilities with the world, however, Ding Fire people can be relentless and unstoppable. Often, they take others by surprise in the revelation of the amount of things they are able to do. More often than not, Ding Fire possesses a lot more talent and intelligence than others give them credit for.

KEY FACTS

- Discreet
- Multi-talented
- Self-effacing
- Rising to the occasion
- Mesmerising

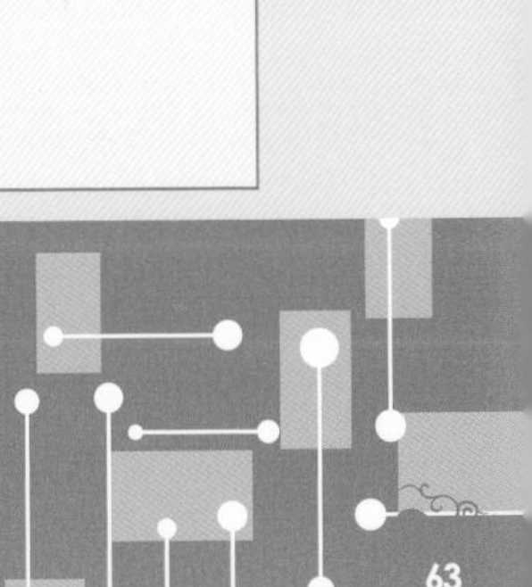

Rules-based

Follow my guidelines... or else!

As leaders, Ding Fire people are very much governed by a proper set of rules or procedures. They take this very seriously, and will not be the kind of leader who will bend the rules as they see fit. They are usually principle-centred. Once the regulations have been set, the Ding Fire leader will adhere to it to a tee.

Ding Fire leaders feel that they earn their sense of authority from having a clear set of principles or rules that they and others can follow. In that sense, the Ding Fire person's leadership is usually free from independent reasoning and will focus heavily on the regulations or formats imposed by external sources.

If the rules that are imposed are strict, then Ding Fire leaders will also have a similarly severe style of management. If the rules are somewhat lax, then the Ding Fire leader will similarly mimic that kind of leadership style in dealing with their team or subordinates.

KEY FACTS ■■■

- Governed by principles
- Less independent reasoning
- Prefers to follow by-the-book
- Does not improvise on leadership styles without consensus

EMPATHETIC
But can be seen as inconsistent

Where their inherent personalities are concerned, Ding Fire people make very considerate leaders. While they may be rigid in adhering to the rules set forth by their company or boss, they also often want to ensure that the people under them are comfortable and fulfilled, and will not go out of their way to make things difficult.

Unfortunately, this can also generate some backlash among their employees. Ding Fire people may be mistaken for being two-faced or wavering because they are sometimes overly considerate for the needs of others. As such, when they are busy trying to help or motivate

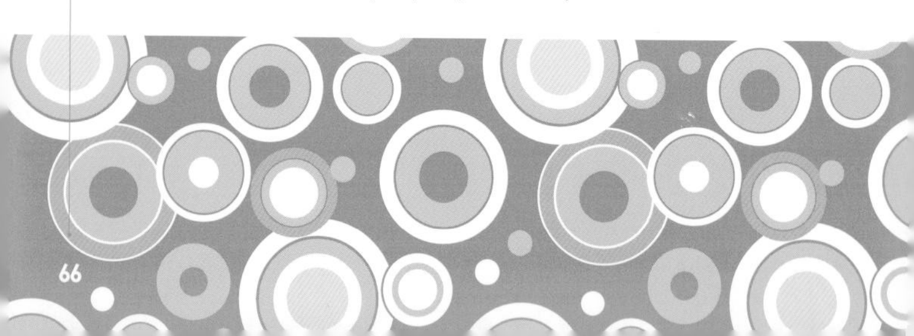

others at their own expense, they don't reveal their true selves.

As such, others will mistakenly conclude at times that theDing Fire person has no inclination or thoughts of their own. Furthermore, this form of excess consideration for their subordinates will have detrimental effects on Ding Fire people themselves. They may become excessively wary or suspicious to the emotions of others, and may react to others accordingly.

KEY FACTS

- Soft spot for others
- Conflicting emotions
- Emotionally unstable
- Often land in 'Damned if you do, damned if you don't' situations
- May be perceived as being 'two-faced'

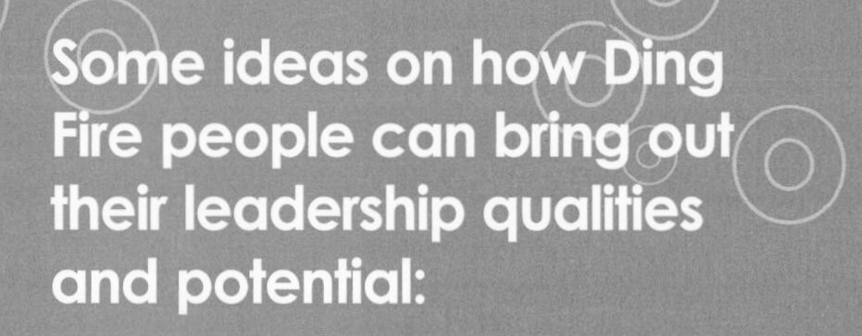

Some ideas on how Ding Fire people can bring out their leadership qualities and potential:

- **Be reasonable about the rules.** Ding Fire people need to be careful about the role played by rules and regulations in their leadership style! Being excessively dependent on playing it by the book may cause them to lose the respect of their employees, or be seen as an unreliable 'candle in the wind!'

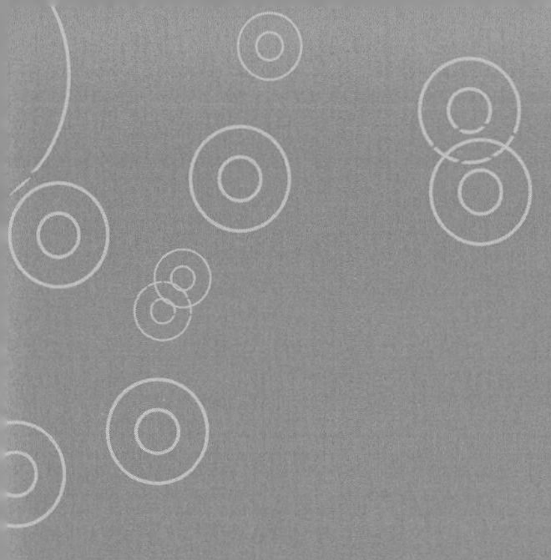

- Learn the rules inside out. If they insist on playing it by the rules, they can still make it better for everyone involved by ensuring that they know what's going on. Study the rules, analyse it, and ensure that they know the rules inside out! And better yet, know what's the exception to the rules. This way, if others object or protest the use of rules, the Ding Fire leader has all the relevant information at the fingertips!

- Read the right books, take the right classes. To improve their leadership skills and become more effective at leading others and guiding them, Ding Fire people will benefit from reading books or magazines that offer versatile management tips. Alternatively, they should consider signing up for a course that will teach them how to apply these skills in practical situations.

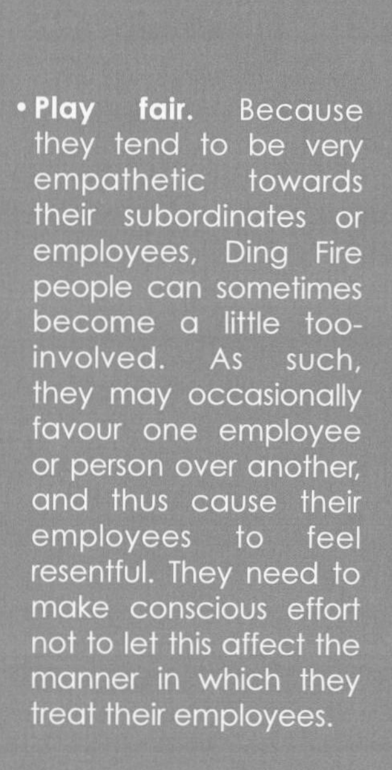

• **Play fair.** Because they tend to be very empathetic towards their subordinates or employees, Ding Fire people can sometimes become a little too-involved. As such, they may occasionally favour one employee or person over another, and thus cause their employees to feel resentful. They need to make conscious effort not to let this affect the manner in which they treat their employees.

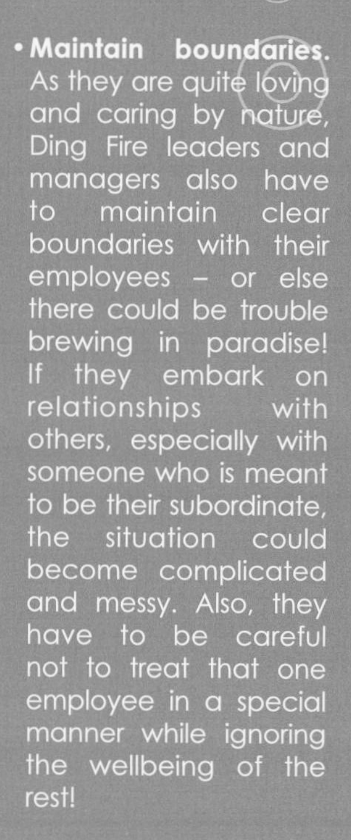

• **Maintain boundaries.** As they are quite loving and caring by nature, Ding Fire leaders and managers also have to maintain clear boundaries with their employees – or else there could be trouble brewing in paradise! If they embark on relationships with others, especially with someone who is meant to be their subordinate, the situation could become complicated and messy. Also, they have to be careful not to treat that one employee in a special manner while ignoring the wellbeing of the rest!

公正

fair

business

BUSINESS ACUMEN

PEOPLE-CENTRED

Putting their customers first

In business, Ding Fire people are the kind of business-owners or entrepreneurs who highly value their clients and customers. They understand that people are central to the success of their enterprise, and will therefore not be the type to take advantage of their customers' trust.

Ding Fire people enjoy nothing more than being able to directly communicate with their clients, and will be very open to receiving comments and feedback. They enjoy receiving their thoughts and learning from

the suggestions given, in the hopes of being able to generate more income and profits.

Because of their naturally empathetic natures, Ding Fire people have an intrinsic talent to be able to understand what their customers want. They will be able to zero in on their customers' desires and identify what it is that is being said – even if it is not being said overtly.

KEY FACTS

- Value their customers desires
- Good communicators
- Understand their customers' needs
- Open to feedback

GOOD DEBATERS

Will argue their way forward!

In terms of marketing and sales, Ding Fire people are able to logically reason their way out of or into any situation. They are very good at crafting good argumentative points and possess strong and superior persuasive powers. They will have the patience to influence their customers and clients toward their point of view.

When faced with any customer or client who proves to be difficult, or a hard-sell, Ding Fire people will often expertly put a pretty spin on things and convince even the most cynical customer of the value

of their products and services. They do this through facts and figures. They are utterly enthusiastic about doing this – which makes it all the better!

Most of the time, this particular tactic is able to win over people and convert casual visitors into loyal customers. However, in situations where the customer or client is equally hard-headed, the reverse effect is possible, and there is a tendency for Ding Fire entrepreneurs to alienate their customers because they're perceived as being too argumentative.

KEY FACTS

- **Logic and reasoning prowess**
- **Loves a good debate**
- **Will present a credible case**
- **Based on facts and figures**

EXPLOSIVE POWER

Wanna be startin' somethin'

As we've talked about before, Ding Fire people look very unassuming and gentle on the outside. However, once their flame is ignited, they can really burn! Once they indulge or immerse themselves in an activity, they tend to go at it whole-heartedly and with full force.

Because Yin Fire represents the flames, a Ding Fire person will totally consume whatever it is they do – they rarely just burn 'halfway' through and stop. And in order to continue burning, they need to consume. That's why Ding Fire people are never idle. They always need to be doing something. They rarely stop

halfway – even if there is a lack of support, or preparation.

It is therefore prudent for Ding Fire people to not act on impulse and to indulge in any form of business until they've done adequate research and preparation. One of the common mistakes of the average Ding Fire person when it comes to business is that they tend to act on impulse or gut feeling as opposed to being adequately prepared. A highly developed Ding Fire person would be more precise and careful before embarking on his/her financial ventures.

KEY FACTS

- **Immerses in full**
- **'Take no prisoners' attitude**

- **Sometimes act on impulse or gut feeling**
- **Restless and tireless**

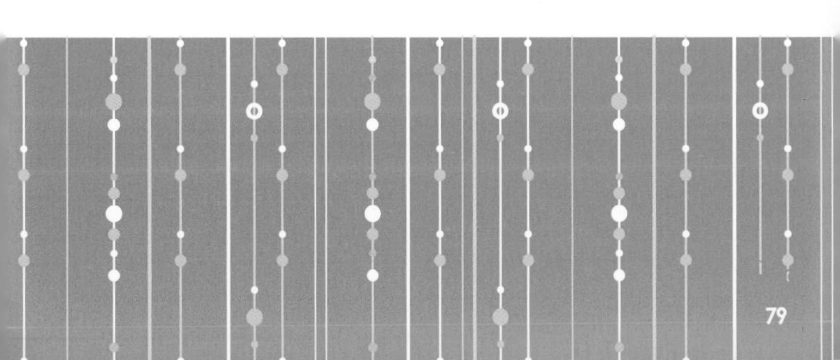

Some ideas on how Ding Fire people can bring out their business potential:

- **Be a direct communicator.** Ding Fire people will shine when their business endeavours require them to communicate directly with other people. They will be able to bring out their strengths in networking and interaction and use it to their benefit in gaining more clients and customers.

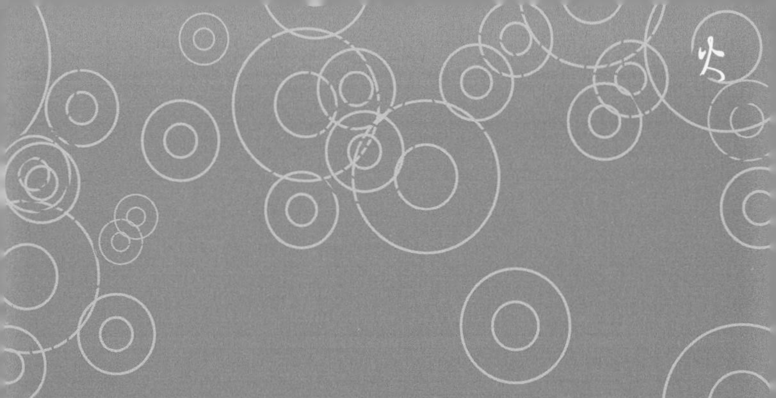

- **Be a listener.** When it comes to listening to their customers, and people in general, and being open and receptive to feedback and comments, Ding Fire people excel admirably. They have a natural tendency to draw out people's confidence, and will always project an air of sincerity and acceptance that will make people feel certain enough to share their deepest reservations.

- **Cultivate your ear for conversation.** Ding Fire people are fantastic in steering an argument, but they can also excel in their business if they know what to listen out for in their customers' comments. Sometimes, it's the unsaid things – or the things conveyed in different words – that have the most significance!

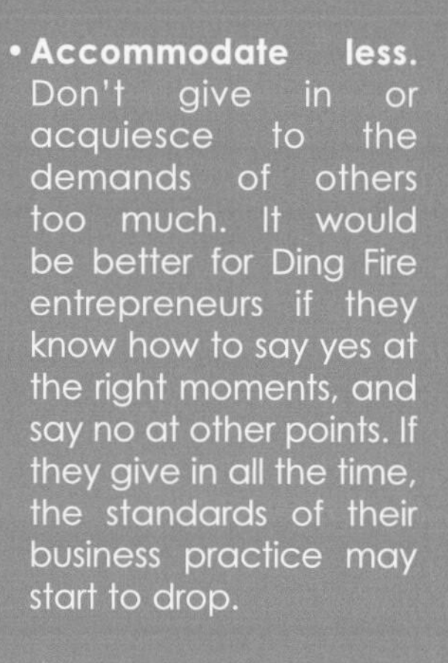

- **Accommodate less.** Don't give in or acquiesce to the demands of others too much. It would be better for Ding Fire entrepreneurs if they know how to say yes at the right moments, and say no at other points. If they give in all the time, the standards of their business practice may start to drop.

- **Brush up on their knowledge.** Ding Fire people are open to gaining new knowledge, and enjoy doing things by the book. As such, for any issue or problem that arises, they will naturally gravitate to learning more about it. This is an interest and an inclination that they should cultivate and nurture, and allow to seep into various other areas as well. They'll be able to grasp things quickly, and the more they learn about best business practices the better it'll be for them.

- **Control ilmpulse.** Before jumping into something in full, first view all the options and details. Try not to adopt a 'burn all bridges' attitude to succeed. Ding Fire people Mmust learn to keep options open.

The Ding Fire Work Character at a Glance:

- You're liable to win Most Popular at the workplace, because you're extremely cordial, courteous, fun-loving and helpful. Even if someone comes to you with the most insane request in the middle of a busy day, you will never have the heart to say, "I'm busy, go away."

- You are also the type to form good relationships at work, because you're good at talking and conversing. People might be surprised that you're able to chat and converse as easily with the CEO or General Manager as you are with the janitor, and everyone else in-between!

- Unlike the sun, which shines brightly as if to announce its presence – "I am HERE!" – you are a gentle, subtle sort of talent. Bit by bit, you will reveal your capabilities to those at work, and allow them to admire you for your abilities in due time. For you, there is no rush.

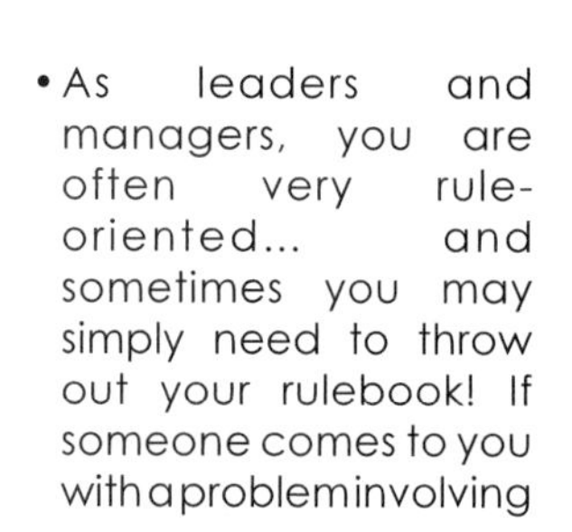

- As leaders and managers, you are often very rule-oriented... and sometimes you may simply need to throw out your rulebook! If someone comes to you with a problem involving an emotionally-manipulative colleague, for example, you can't possibly flip through the pages of a book to find the solution! A practical problem requires a practical solution.

- You will be able to talk up a storm if you want to, and so you're able to be genuinely persuasive and convincing when it comes to goading a customer or client into buying a product, or signing up for a service. You're blessed with the innate ability to listen as much as you talk.

- Once you've managed to convince a customer to buy your products, you have the ability to win over their lasting loyalty.

RELATIONSHIPS

同伴
companion

FRIENDS & COLLEAGUES

NEEDY

Can't live if living is without you...

Ding Fire people take care of those around them. And similarly, they expect to be taken care of. They yearn for some TLC (tender, loving care) from their partners. Somewhat like toddlers and infants when it comes to interpersonal relationships, Ding Fire people can prove to be exceptionally needy and dependent when it comes down to relationships.

They like to be pampered and nurtured, and sometimes this can be a little overwhelming to their closest friends and confidantes. If they don't get the attention they want from others, or if they feel that their friends ignore them

or don't acknowledge them as they should, then they lose their good spirits easily and can fall into a foul temper.

As such, they may sometimes put on their "Woe is me" attitude and regale their friends not with tales of entertainment, but with sorry tales of their problems and issues. They try to gain attention from others by arousing pity and concern; but if they overdo this, they start to turn people off more than anything else.

KEY FACTS

- Needs Tender, Loving, Care
- Clingy
- Attention-seeking

- Throws pity parties

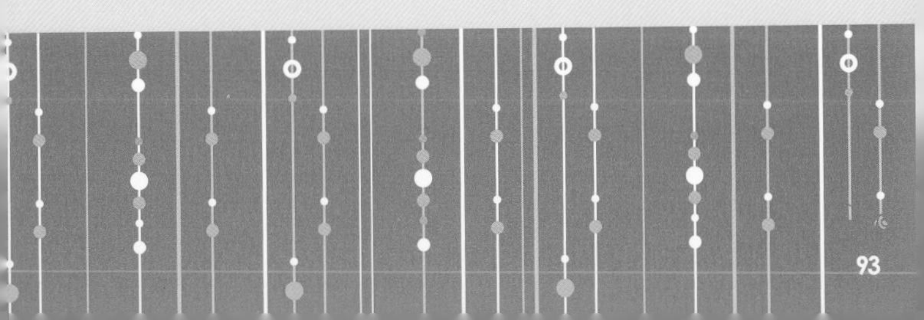

OLD IS GOLD
Respecting their elders

Ding Fire people have a special affinity for their elders, and accord them a due mark of respect. They enjoy being around their elders and people who are generally older than them, because they feel that there is plenty to learn from these wiser souls who have lived more years on this planet.

They find it easier to accept the will and authority of people older than them, and will have no problems forming friendships with older people. At the workplace, Ding Fire people will typically have an older mentor to whom they turn for wise counsel, advice, and general discussion and exchange of ideas.

However, when the tables are turned and younger people come to them for

advice, an average Ding Fire person is quick to lose his/her patience. They don't like to be the ones whom others turn to; instead, they prefer to have the comforts of turning to their elders without the burden of being looked up to by those younger than them. Sometimes it's not really about the age, but the mental maturity of those with whom they deal with. As such, you'll find that Ding Fire people often enjoy good relationships with people who are older (or wiser) than they are.

KEY FACTS

- Enjoys the company of older or wiser people
- Look up to who are more knowledgeable
- Respect their elders' wisdom
- More comfortable with older people

WARY

Cagey about getting close

Because Ding Fire people are very sensitive, and because their moods and temperaments tend to flicker like candlelight, their relationships with others are somewhat complicated. This can come as a surprise, since Ding Fire people can be genuinely devoted and loving once they really trust and like someone.

They don't have the clear-as-bell belief in themselves of being liked for the simple reason that they're likeable! As such, it's a long hard road for them to forming true friendships with people, because they always wonder why it is that anyone else will like them.

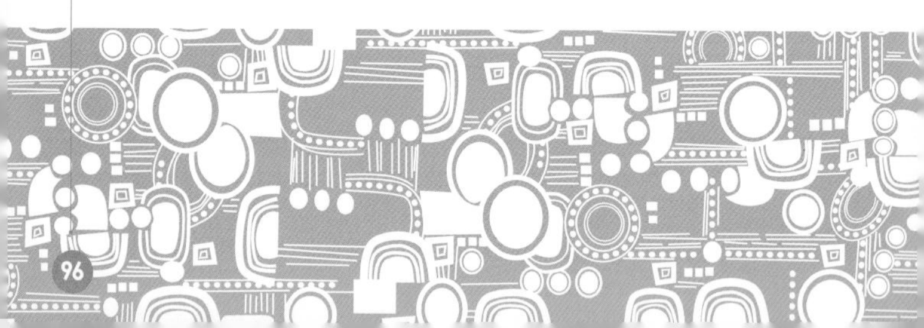

Many Ding Fire people are often suspicious for the motives behind a person's interest in them, and will tend to miss out on the really good connections because they're spending too much time being guarded and mistrustful. Protecting themselves becomes the primary concern, and as such many potentially beautiful friendships and acquaintances are sidelined.

KEY FACTS

- **Apprehensive and suspicious**
- **Afraid of getting too close**
- **Erecting barriers with others**
- **Will have trouble fully trusting friends**

Some ideas on how Ding Fire people can bring out their potential in relationships:

- **Reign in the sarcasm.** Ding Fire people can be sarcastic and snappy to people when they're less than happy – and if they really dislike someone, they can be quite cold. Their fire is instantly snuffed out! However, they should bear in mind the maxim, "Do unto others as you would have others do unto you." There is always a relationship of cause and effect in relationships!

- **Take care of themselves.** The less they need to rely on other people for their own happiness – whether for actual day-to-day help in the business of living, or for moral support and encouragement – the more they will able to appreciate individuals for who they are. When they know they don't need others around all the time to make them happy, then they will stop assuming that others also want them around for help.

- **Understand that emotions will ALWAYS change.** Once they realise this, Ding Fire people will be able to accept that the changes of emotions don't have to dictate how they behave and react to others. More important, changes in emotions don't have to dictate how they CHOOSE to feel about things. This will affect their relationships significantly – in a good way.

- **Up the fun factor in groups.** Ding Fire people can participate more in group activities that are fun and lighthearted. They love to the center of attention. For example, classes on ballroom dancing, or any other form of dance. Sports and athletic activities like martial arts, volleyball, badminton, or even soothing physical activities like Tai Qi, yoga or jogging groups will help them relate to others more naturally.

- **Learn to relax!** They should indulge in any sort of activities that will calm down and slow down their moods and make them less agitated. When their mind and spirits are calm, they will be better inclined to approach their interpersonal relationships with the same grace and ease with which they approach learning.

The Ding Fire 'People' Character at a Glance:

- Why drive yourself around, pay your own bills, or cook your own food if there's someone else to do it? It's not that you like to take advantage of people or make them work for your affections – you just love the feeling of being taken care of!

- You are very demonstrative of your affections to the people to whom you're close, and will go out of your way to ensure that they feel happy and comfortable. For that reason, when you make friends, whether in the workplace or out, they tend to have a place in your life for a very long time.
- If you have a stomach ache, it doesn't really matter whether or not it's mild or severe, but the whole world will have to know about it! You waste no time in sharing your pains and troubles with your friends, and see no problem in gaining a few sympathy points while you're at it.

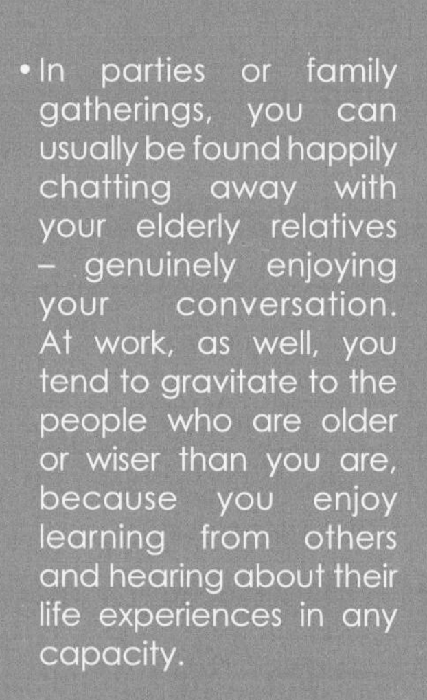

- In parties or family gatherings, you can usually be found happily chatting away with your elderly relatives – genuinely enjoying your conversation. At work, as well, you tend to gravitate to the people who are older or wiser than you are, because you enjoy learning from others and hearing about their life experiences in any capacity.

- You tend to erect walls around yourself to prevent people from taking advantage of you. But face it, Ding Fire, you're extremely lovable and others simply can't stay away. Stop questioning why others want to be friends with you, and simply allow them to do so!

- Your quick-thinking abilities allow you to respond with sarcasm most of the time, but while you're congratulating yourself on a particularly witty aside, the people in your line of fire could be trying to hold back tears.
- You have a fun, light-hearted, sparkling side to your personality that comes out when you're comfortable doing something you enjoy, or are at play. So cultivate that attitude by scheduling in some serious FUN TIME with friends and colleagues into your planner.

WEALTH

經濟
economic

MONEY MATTERS

CRAVES DIRECTION

Expert advice is gold

Ding Fire people are the type of people who will find expert financial advice to be heaven-sent, because they place a lot of value on professional expertise and consultation. This is all the more the case when the subject in question has to do with money! They prefer to be guided and shown the way. If possible, they will try to find a way not to think about complex financial matters – especially if they don't have prior knowledge on the subject.

As we've already come to realise, most Ding Fire people feel better when they can rely on others and depend on others. In the same vein, in matters of wealth and financial management, they

would rather wholly surrender the nitty-gritty details to their financial advisors or consultants instead of figuring it out on their own. For that reason, Ding Fire people can be quite easily taken for a ride where financial matters are concerned – if they are not careful.

KEY FACTS

- **Reliant on expert advice**
- **Can be gullible**
- **Prefer being guided on money matters**
- **Feel better being directed by others**

This is because they trust someone implicitly if they feel they can trust his or her methods of financial planning, not taking into account the variable factor – characters. Plenty of people peddling financial advice are intellectually and professionally adept, but may have shady characters and ill intentions. This can be quite dangerous and costly in the end for quite a number of Ding Fire people, as they are prone to being cheated for thinking that everyone is as honest as they are!

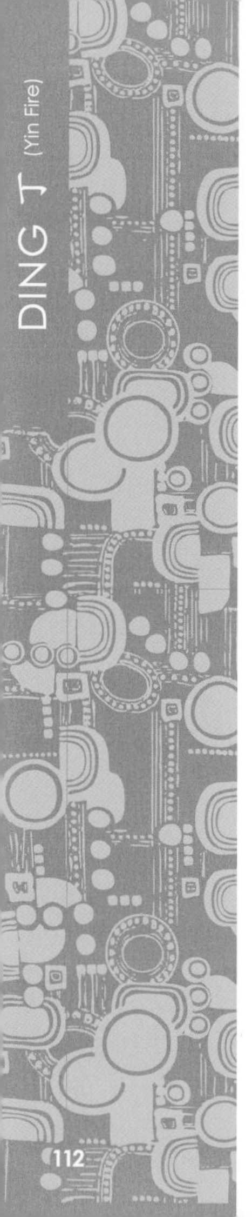

SHOW ME THE FACTS!

Preferring facts and figures

Despite their perchance for wanting to be guided and shown their way, Ding Fire people place a high premium on expert analysis. As such, they *want* to trust professional advice and expertise, but they will only surrender their beliefs to a professional financial manager or consultant once they're assured that the methods are infallible. In other words, they believe in 'facts and figures.'

Ding Fire people are unlikely the types to light a fire and hold hands to chant some incantations for wealth. They are also not given to peering into a crystal ball and hoping for the answer to appear. Ding Fire appreciates the FACTS. They have a tremendous amount of respect proper methods and

methodology (they do have meticulous natures, remember!).

As such, they have the utmost respect and regard for financial analysis that is grounded in facts, proofs, and numbers. Even if they don't quite understand what the methods or systems are like, they will appreciate its value and will honour the advice of people who practice a proper, structured form of financial management. For this reason, you can only pull the wool over Ding Fire's eyes if you've managed to convince them of your methods of analysis.

KEY FACTS

- **Scrupulous**
- **Respects proper analysis**
- **Not into quick schemes**
- **Will demand proper methods and proofs**

投資

investment

Quick Tips on Managing Finances:

- *Learn more about the analyses that are related to financial management*
- *If you want to trust other implicitly when it comes to financial advice, know what you are trusting!*
- *Vet and screen through all potential financial consultants thoroughly*
- *Be more circumspect and less naïve when it comes to trusting others*

Some ideas on how Ding Fire people can improve their money management skills and financial acumen:

- **Hit the books!** There are a wealth of books, courses, and training programs available these days on the subject of financial management. In this day and age, none of us can afford not to know the ins-and-outs of a financial management process, especially Ding Fire! Doing the proper research and homework will greatly increase Ding Fire's sense of confidence.

- **Study all aspects.** Ding Fire is, by nature, a Day Master that enjoys learning and expanding its knowledge. As such, they should make an effort to learn EVERYTHING related to their preferred form of financial investment, from the theory and application, right down to all its various elements like politics, economy, and history, and various other factors.

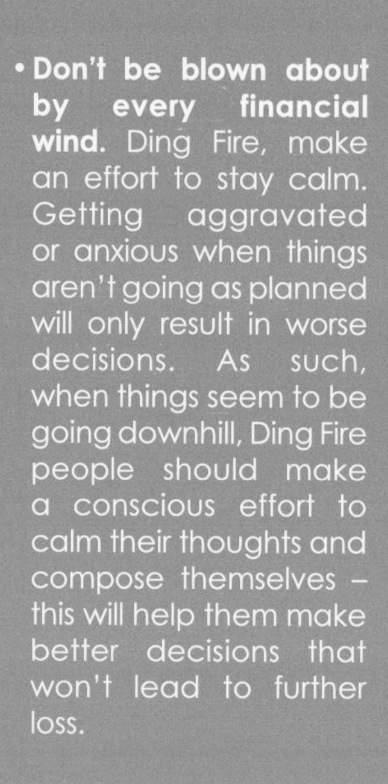

- **Don't be blown about by every financial wind.** Ding Fire, make an effort to stay calm. Getting aggravated or anxious when things aren't going as planned will only result in worse decisions. As such, when things seem to be going downhill, Ding Fire people should make a conscious effort to calm their thoughts and compose themselves – this will help them make better decisions that won't lead to further loss.

- **Be flexible.** Ding Fire people will feel more comfortable once they know that there are more options – and they should therefore make it an imperative to know all about the options that are available! That way, they won't feel like they're *stuck* in one situation or investment. For example, if the stock market becomes volatile and unstable, they should realise they have the option to transfer their funds to a fixed deposit.

- **Realise that money isn't everything.** It will help to realise that money is not the only thing that makes the world go round – although it does play a pretty big role! They need to learn to enjoy the journey.

The Ding Fire 'Money' Character at a Glance:

- As a Ding Fire person, you crave a sense of safety from being taken care of by others. This is all well and good in most cases, but in matters of money, you need to RESIST the urge for trusting another person's financial advice implicitly. Financial literacy is something a Ding Fire person should try to obtain as early as possible in life.
- That being said, however, it must be noted that you don't trust just any Tom, Dick, or Harry with a finance degree. You have precise and meticulous standards of criteria, but the bad part is, once you've approved of someone's methods and standards of procedure, you tend to trust implicitly.

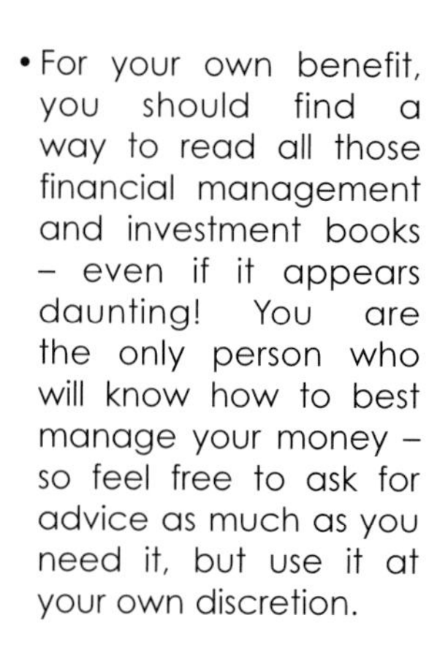

- For your own benefit, you should find a way to read all those financial management and investment books – even if it appears daunting! You are the only person who will know how to best manage your money – so feel free to ask for advice as much as you need it, but use it at your own discretion.
- You have the ability to understand investment theories from the inside out – so if you learn all there is to know about investment for yourself, who knows... YOU might be the investment consultant that everyone turns to in the near future! In other words, become the financial expert that you so admire.

- Develop an interest in all things related to finance. Study the power of money. Learn to see money as a score card and play it as a game. You, Ding Fire, have the intellectual capabilities for this as well.

Further Your BaZi Knowledge
Recommended Reading and Courses

Must-have BaZi Basics!

BaZi – The Destiny Code provides complete beginners knowledge on the fundamentals of BaZi in clear, easy-to-understand language and vivid examples, while BaZi – The Destiny Code Revealed is an in-depth resource on advanced BaZi principles and theories.

1) BaZi – The Destiny Code

2) BaZi – The Destiny Code Revealed

WWW.MASTERYACADEMY.COM/ESTORE

Study BaZi from the Comforts of Your Home

Supplement your BaZi studies from home with our online courses. Video lectures by Joey Yap, combined with slide presentations and notes, provide you with a complete BaZi learning experience. All without having to step outside your door!

Study BaZi at the Mastery Academy

Embark on BaZi classes at the Mastery Academy with Joey Yap and our team of professional instructors. Learn the ancient techniques and secrets in an intimate, friendly setting, aided by professional teaching tools and workbooks. Practical training and a conducive learning environment!

Module One – Intensive Foundation Course
Module Two – Practitioners Course
Module Three – Advanced Practitioners Course
Module Four – BaZi Mastery

About Joey Yap

Joey Yap is the Founder and Master Trainer of the Mastery Academy of Chinese Metaphysics, a global organization devoted to the teaching of Feng Shui, BaZi, Mian Xiang and other Chinese Metaphysics subjects. He is also the Chief Consultant of Yap Global Consulting, an international consulting firm specialising in Feng Shui and Chinese Astrology services and audits.

He is the bestselling author of over 25 books, including ***Stories and Lessons on Feng Shui***, ***BaZi – The Destiny Code, Mian Xiang – Discover Face Reading***, ***Feng Shui for Homebuyers Series***, and ***Pure Feng Shui,*** which was released by an international publisher.

He is also the producer of the first comprehensive reference source of Chinese Metaphysics, ***The Chinese Metaphysics Compendium***, a compilation of all the essential formulas and applications known and practiced in Chinese Metaphysics today. He has since produced various other reference books and workbooks to aid students in their study and practice of Chinese Metaphysics subjects.

An avid proponent of technology being the way forward in disseminating knowledge of Chinese Metaphysics, Joey has developed, among others, the ***BaZi Ming Pan 2.0 Software*** and the ***Xuan Kong Flying Stars Feng Shui Software***. This passion for fusing the best of modern technology with the best of classical studies lead him to create one of the pioneer online schools for Chinese Metaphysics education, the Mastery Academy E-Learning Centre (www.maelearning.com).

In addition to being a regular guest on various international radio and TV shows, Joey has also written columns for leading newspapers, as well as having contributed articles for various international magazines and publications. He has been featured in many popular publications and media including *Time International*, *Forbes International*, the *International Herald Tribune*, and Bloomberg TV, and was selected as one of Malaysia Tatler's 'Most Influential People in Malaysia' in 2008.

A naturally engaging speaker, Joey has presented to clients like Citibank, HSBC, IBM, Microsoft, Sime Darby, Bloomberg, HP, Samsung, Mah Sing, Nokia, Dijaya, and Standard Chartered.

Joey has also hosted his own TV series, *Discovering Feng Shui with Joey Yap*, and appeared on Malaysia's Astro TV network's *Walking the Dragons with Joey Yap*.

Author's personal websites : **www.joeyyap.com** I **www.fengshuilogy.com** (Personal Blog)
Academy websites : **www.masteryacademy.com** I **www.maelearning.com**
Follow Joey's regular updates on Twitter: **www.twitter.com/joeyyap**

EDUCATION

The Mastery Academy of Chinese Metaphysics: the first choice for practitioners and aspiring students of the art and science of Chinese Classical Feng Shui and Astrology.

For thousands of years, Eastern knowledge has been passed from one generation to another through the system of discipleship. A venerated master would accept suitable individuals at a young age as his disciples, and informally through the years, pass on his knowledge and skills to them. His disciples in turn, would take on their own disciples, as a means to perpetuate knowledge or skills.

This system served the purpose of restricting the transfer of knowledge to only worthy honourable individuals and ensuring that outsiders or Westerners would not have access to thousands of years of Eastern knowledge, learning and research.

However, the disciple system has also resulted in Chinese Metaphysics and Classical Studies lacking systematic teaching methods. Knowledge garnered over the years has not been accumulated in a concise, systematic manner, but scattered amongst practitioners, each practicing his/her knowledge, art and science, in isolation.

The disciple system, out of place in today's modern world, endangers the advancement of these classical fields that continue to have great relevance and application today.

At the Mastery Academy of Chinese Metaphysics, our Mission is to bring Eastern Classical knowledge in the fields of metaphysics, Feng Shui and Astrology sciences and the arts to the world. These Classical teachings and knowledge, previously shrouded in secrecy and passed on only through the discipleship system, are adapted into structured learning, which can easily be understood, learnt and mastered. Through modern learning methods, these renowned ancient arts, sciences and practices can be perpetuated while facilitating more extensive application and understanding of these classical subjects.

The Mastery Academy espouses an educational philosophy that draws from the best of the East and West. It is the world's premier educational institution for the study of Chinese Metaphysics Studies offering a wide range and variety of courses, ensuring that students have the opportunity to pursue their preferred field of study and enabling existing practitioners and professionals to gain cross-disciplinary knowledge that complements their current field of practice.

Courses at the Mastery Academy have been carefully designed to ensure a comprehensive yet compact syllabus. The modular nature of the courses enables students to immediately begin to put their knowledge into practice while pursuing continued study of their field and complementary fields. Students thus have the benefit of developing and gaining practical experience in tandem with the expansion and advancement of their theoretical knowledge.

Students can also choose from a variety of study options, from a distance learning program, the Homestudy Series, that enables study at one's own pace or intensive foundation courses and compact lecture-based courses, held in various cities around the world by Joey Yap or our licensed instructors. The Mastery Academy's faculty and make-up is international in nature, thus ensuring that prospective students can attend courses at destinations nearest to their country of origin or with a licensed Mastery Academy instructor in their home country.

The Mastery Academy provides 24x7 support to students through its Online Community, with a variety of tools, documents, forums and e-learning materials to help students stay at the forefront of research in their fields and gain invaluable assistance from peers and mentoring from their instructors.

MASTERY ACADEMY
OF CHINESE METAPHYSICS

www.masteryacademy.com

MALAYSIA

19-3, The Boulevard, Mid Valley City, 59200 Kuala Lumpur, Malaysia
Tel : +603-2284 8080 Fax : +603-2284 1218 Email : info@masteryacademy.com

SINGAPORE

14, Robinson Road # 13-00, Far East Finance Building, Singapore 048545
Tel : +65-6494 9147 Email : singapore@masteryacademy.com

Australia, Austria, Canada, China, Croatia, Cyprus, Czech Republic, Denmark, France, Germany, Greece Hungary, India, Italy, Kazakhstan, Malaysia, Netherlands (Holland), New Zealand, Philippines, Poland, Rus Federation, Singapore, Slovenia, South Africa, Switzerland, Turkey, U.S.A., Ukraine, United Kingdom

Mastery Academy around the world

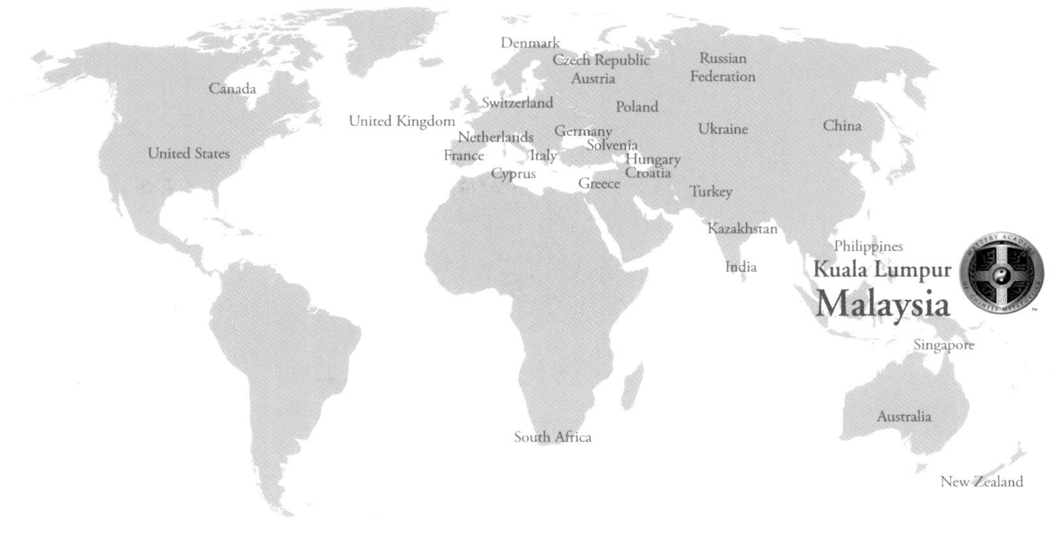

Feng Shui Consultations

For Residential Properties
- Initial Land/Property Assessment
- Residential Feng Shui Consultations
- Residential Land Selection
- End-to-End Residential Consultation

For Commercial Properties
- Initial Land/Property Assessment
- Commercial Feng Shui Consultations
- Commercial Land Selection
- End-to-End Commercial Consultation

For Property Developers
- End-to-End Consultation
- Post-Consultation Advisory Services
- Panel Feng Shui Consultant

For Property Investors
- Your Personal Feng Shui Consultant
- Tailor-Made Packages

For Memorial Parks & Burial Sites
- Yin House Feng Shui

BaZi Consultations

Personal Destiny Analysis
- Personal Destiny Analysis for Individuals
- Children's BaZi Analysis
- Family BaZi Analysis

Strategic Analysis for Corporate Organizations
- Corporate BaZi Consultations
- BaZi Analysis for Human Resource Management

Entrepreneurs & Business Owners
- BaZi Analysis for Entrepreneurs

Career Pursuits
- BaZi Career Analysis

Relationships
- Marriage and Compatibility Analysis
- Partnership Analysis

For Everyone
- Annual BaZi Forecast
- Your Personal BaZi Coach**Personal Destiny Analysis**
- Personal Destiny Analysis for Individuals

Date Selection Consultations

- **Marriage Date Selection**
- **Caesarean Birth Date Selection**
- **House-Moving Date Selection**
- **Renovation & Groundbreaking Dates**
- **Signing of Contracts**
- **Official Openings**
- **Product Launches**

Yi Jing Assessment

A Time-Tested, Accurate Science

- With a history predating 4 millennia, the Yi Jing - or Classic of Change - is one of the oldest Chinese texts surviving today. Its purpose as an oracle, in predicting the outcome of things, is based on the variables of Time, Space and Specific Events.

- A Yi Jing Assessment provides specific answers to any specific questions you may have about a specific event or endeavor. This is something that a Destiny Analysis would not be able to give you.

Basically, what a Yi Jing Assessment does is focus on only ONE aspect or item at a particular point in your life, and give you a calculated prediction of the details that will follow suit, if you undertake a particular action. It gives you an insight into a situation, and what course of action to take in order to arrive at a satisfactory outcome at the end of the day.

Please Contact YGC for a personalized Yi Jing Assessment!

Easy Guide on Face Reading

All you need to know about the Eyes, Eyebrows, Mouth, Nose and Ears.

Joey Yap's brand new Face Reading Essentials Series are easy, fast, and effective guides for beginners, enthusiasts, and the curious. Learn to read your face by identifying the facial features on your own face, and the faces of the people around you.

These are EASY, FAST and EFFECTIVE guides for beginners, enthusiasts, and the curious. Make first impressions work for you by applying Face Reading skills to understand the personality and character of the person standing in front of you, whether at work, in business meetings, on a date, or anywhere else!

Educational Tools & Software

Xuan Kong Flying Stars Feng Shui Software

The Essential Application for Enthusiasts and Professionals

Highlights of the software include:

- Natal Flying Stars
- Annual Flying Stars
- Monthly Flying Stars
- Flying Stars Integration
- 81 Flying Stars Combinations
- 24 Mountains
- Dual-View Format

All charts will be are printable and configurable, and can be saved for future editing. Also, you'll be able to export your charts into most image file formats like jpeg, bmp, and gif.

Mini Feng Shui Compass

The Mini Feng Shui Compass is a self-aligning compass that is not only light at 100gms but also built sturdily to ensure it will be convenient to use anywhere. The rings on the Mini Feng Shui Compass are bi-lingual and incorporate the 24 Mountain Rings that is used in your traditional Luo Pan.

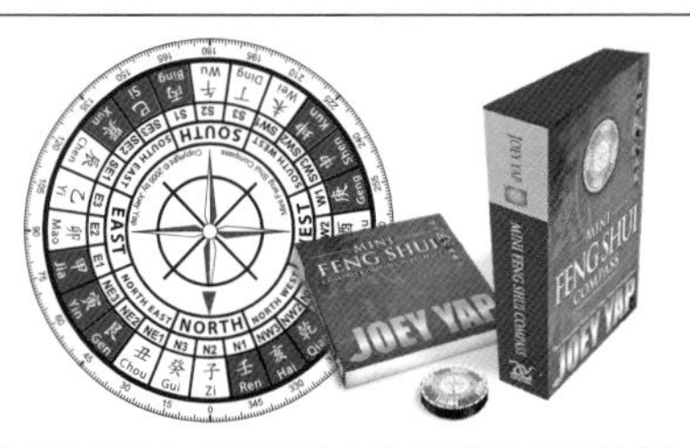

BaZi Ming Pan Software Version 2.0

Professional Four Pillars Calculator for Destiny Analysis

The BaZi Ming Pan Version 2.0 Professional Four Pillars Calculator for Destiny Analysis is the most technically advanced software of its kind in the world today. It allows even those without any knowledge of BaZi to generate their own BaZi Charts, and provides virtually every detail required to undertake a comprehensive Destiny Analysis.

Joey Yap Feng Shui Template Set

The Set comprises 3 basic templates: The Basic Feng Shui Template, 8 Mansions Feng Shui Template, and the Flying Stars Feng Shui Template.

Main Features:

- Easy-to-use, simple, and straightforward
- Small and portable; each template measuring only 5" x 5"
- Additional 8 Mansions and Flying Stars Reference Rings
- Handy companion booklet with usage tips and examples

Feng Shui for Homebuyers DVD Series

In these DVDs, Joey will guide you on how to customise your home to maximise the Feng Shui potential of your property and gain the full benefit of improving your health, wealth and love life using the 9 Palace Grid. He will show you how to go about applying the classical applications of the Life Gua and House Gua techniques to get attuned to your Sheng Qi (positive energies).

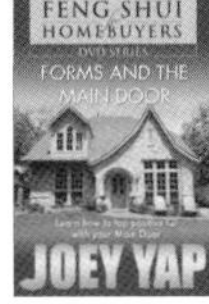

Accelerate Your Face Reading Skills With Joey Yap's Face Reading Revealed DVD Series

In these highly entertaining DVDs, Joey will help you answer all these questions and more. You will be able to ascertain the underlying meaning of moles, birthmarks or even the type of your hair in Face Reading. Joey will also reveal the guidelines to help you foster better and stronger relationships with your loved ones through Mian Xiang.

Discover Feng Shui with Joey Yap (TV Series) - Set of 4 DVDS

Informative and entertaining, classical Feng Shui comes alive in *Discover Feng Shui with Joey Yap!*

Own the series that national channel 8TV did a re-run of in 2005, today!

Book: Feng Shui for Homebuyers Series

Feng Shui For Homebuyers - Exterior
(English & Chinese versions)

Feng Shui for Homebuyers - Interior

Feng Shui for Apartment Buyers - Home Owners

Book: Stories and Lessons on Feng Shui Series

Stories and Lessons on Feng Shui
(English & Chinese versions)

More Stories and Lessons on Feng Shui

Even More Stories and Lessons on Feng Shui

Continue Your Journey with Joey Yap's Books

Walking the Dragons

Your Aquarium Here

The Art of Date Selection: Personal Date Selection

Mian Xiang - Discover Face Reading
(English & Chinese versions)

The Ten Thousand Year Calendar

Xuan Kong: Flying Stars Feng Shui

Elevate Your Feng Shui Skills With Joey Yap's Home Study Course And Educational DVDs

Xuan Kong Vol.1
An Advanced Feng Shui Home Study Course

Feng Shui for Period 8 - (DVD)

Xuan Kong Flying Stars Beginners Workshop - (DVD)

BaZi Four Pillars of Destiny Beginners Workshop - (DVD)

Interested in learning MORE about Feng Shui? Advance Your Feng Shui Knowledge with the Mastery Academy Courses.

Feng Shui Mastery Series™
LIVE COURSES (MODULES ONE TO FOUR)

The Feng Shui Mastery Series comprises Feng Shui Mastery Modules 1, 2, 3, and 4. It is a program that introduces students to the theories, principles, analyses, and interpretations of classical Feng Shui. It is a thorough, comprehensive program that covers important theories from various classical Feng Shui systems including Ba Zhai, San Yuan, San He, and Xuan Kong.

Xuan Kong Mastery Series™
LIVE COURSES (MODULES ONE TO THREE)

* Advanced Courses For Master Practitioners

The Xuan Kong Mastery Series allows students to take their introductory steps into the captivating world of this potent and powerful science. While Classical Feng Shui is always about the study of Location and Direction, Xuan Kong factors in the concept of Time into the equation as well. This course that will expose students to the extremely advanced techniques and formulas based upon those that were used by the ancient masters, as derived from the classics.It paves the way for students to specialize in the intelligent and strategic allocation of Qi, allowing them to literally manipulate Qi to assist in their life endeavours.

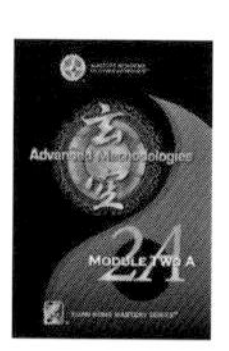

Mian Xiang Mastery Series™

LIVE COURSES (MODULES ONE AND TWO)

As one of the time-tested Five Arts (Wu Xing) of Chinese Metaphysics, Mian Xiang falls under the study of the physiognomy of the features, contours, shapes and hues of the face. In Mian Xiang, however, a person's face is more than what he or she shows the world; it's also a virtual map of this person's potential and destiny in life.

The Mian Xiang Mastery Series comprises Module 1 and Module 2 to allow students to learn this ancient art in a thorough, detailed manner. Each module has a carefully-developed syllabus that allows students to get acquainted with the fundamentals of Mian Xiang before moving on to the more intricate theories and principles that will enable them to practice Mian Xiang with greater depth and complexity.

Ze Ri Mastery Series™

LIVE COURSES (MODULES ONE AND TWO)

The ZeRi Mastery Series, or Date Selection, comprise two modules: ZeRi Mastery Series Module 1 and ZeRi Mastery Series Module 2. This program provides students with a thorough introduction to the art of Date Selection both for Personal and Feng Shui purposes. Both modules provide a fundamental grounding in all the rudimentary basics and allow you to move from the more straightforward techniques in Module 1 to the more sophisticated methods of Xuan Kong Da Gua in Module 2 with ease and confidence.

Yi Jing Mastery Series™

LIVE COURSES (MODULES ONE AND TWO)

'Yi' relates to change. Indeed, flux - or continuous change - is the key concept of the Yi Jing. Change is the only constant in life, and there is no exception to this rule. Evolution, transformation, alteration - call it by any other name, its effects are still far-reaching and encompasses every law - natural or manmade - known to our universe.

The Yi Jing Mastery Series provides an introductory look into the basics and fundamentals of Yi Jing thought and theory. As the Yi Jing functioned as an ancient Chinese oracle thousands of years ago, this Module will explore Yi Jing as a science of divination and probe the ways in which the concept of 'change' plays a big part in Yi Jing. Together both modules aim to give casual and serious Yi Jing enthusiasts a serious insight into one of the most important philosophical treatises in ancient Chinese thought.

Feng Shui for Life

Feng Shui for life is a 5-day course designed for the Feng Shui beginner to learn how to apply practical Feng Shui in day-to-day living. It is a culmination of powerful tools and techniques that allows you to gain quick proficiency in Classical Feng Shui.

Mastery Academy courses are conducted around the world. Find out when will Joey Yap be in your area by visiting **www.masteryacademy.com** or call our office at **+603-2284 8080**.

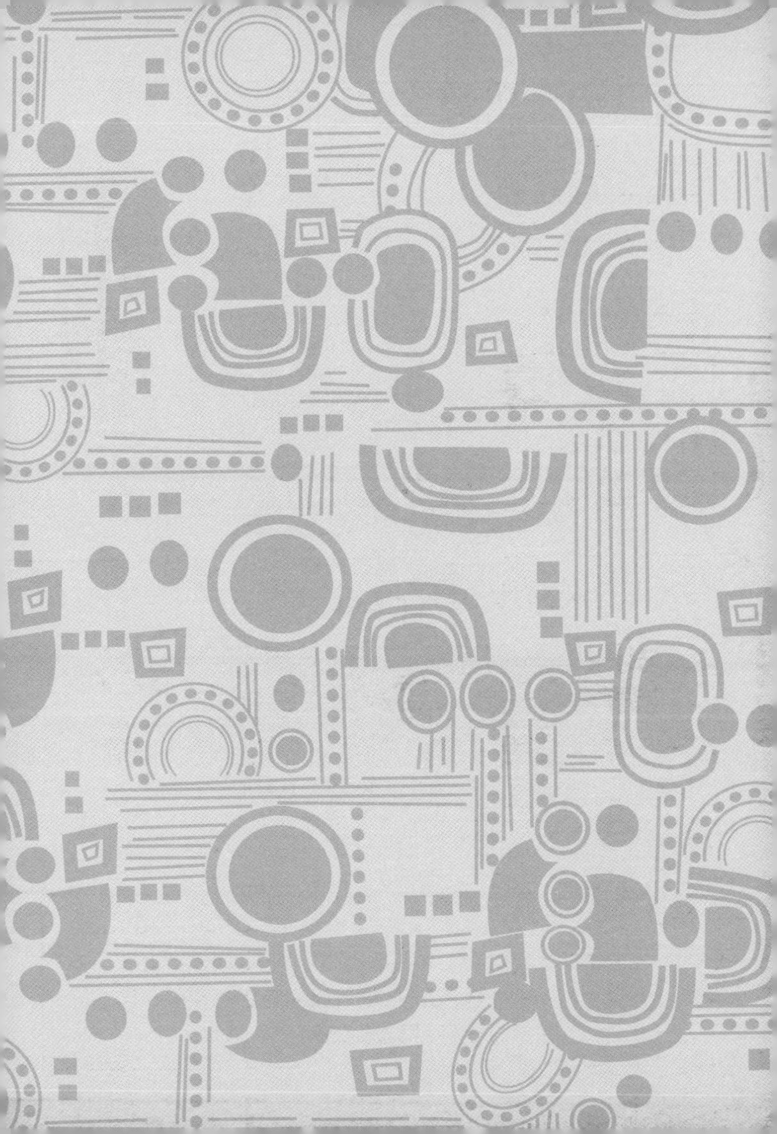

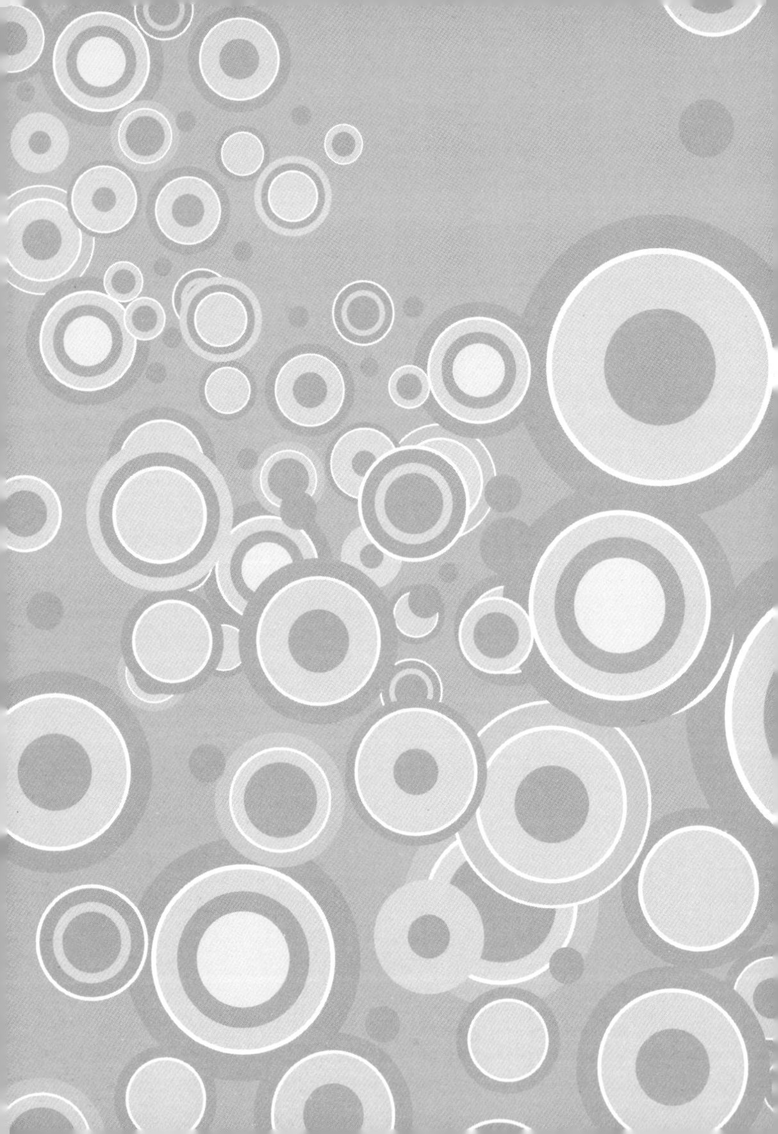